OLD GODS

OLD GODS

CONOR KERR

NIGHTWOOD EDITIONS

2023

Nightwood Editions
P.O. Box 1779
Gibsons, BC VON 1V0
Canada
www.nightwoodeditions.com

COVER DESIGN: Angela Yen
TYPESETTING: Carleton Wilson

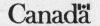

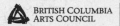

Nightwood Editions acknowledges the support of the Canada Council for the Arts,
the Government of Canada, and the Province of British Columbia through the BC Arts Council.

This book has been produced on 100% post-consumer recycled, ancient-forest-free paper,
processed chlorine-free and printed with vegetable-based dyes.

Printed and bound in Canada.

LIBRARY AND ARCHIVES CANADA CATALOGUING IN PUBLICATION

Title: Old gods / Conor Kerr.
Names: Kerr, Conor, author.
Description: Poems.
Identifiers: Canadiana (print) 20220481768 | Canadiana (ebook) 20220481814 |
    ISBN 9780889714465 (softcover) | ISBN 9780889714472 (EPUB)
Classification: LCC PS8621.E7636 O43 2023 | DDC C811/.6—dc23

For Sam

I rest in the waves of prairie grasses
On the lonesome.
Play me an old country song
Scatter me here and there.
I want to hear the thunder of bison
the patter of dancing sage grouse.
The wind is singing to me now.
The wind is calling me home.
From this hilltop I can see
All the prairie stretched out
A map of possibility.
That I'll ride across forever
Beside my ancestors
Beside those who are yet to come.

Contents

I. JUST PASSING THROUGH

II. MÉTIS MAGIC

III. OLD GODS

I.
JUST PASSING THROUGH

Old Hunting Dogs

Years ago, we scattered my grandfather's ashes in an old, abandoned settler graveyard a hundred klicks south of Moose Jaw on the east shore of Old Wives Lake. There are a couple old stones, buried inside an overgrown caragana bush, engraved with Swedish names and places of birth. I wonder what those early settlers thought about when they died in their early thirties far from their homelands. They were younger than I am now. Did they question what the hell they were doing in a place like this? Did they think about the waterways, mountains and old cities of Sweden with the same longing that I have for endless prairie grasses? Did they wish to be back under familiar stars? Do their descendants know that they're buried here or are they forgotten? Maybe they built their homestead here because of the way Old Wives Lake kicks up salt on a westerly and carries it in the air? Or maybe they just ended up here because of a failed promise of colonial expansion from a government who would and will never give two shits about the prairie. But I highly doubt that they ever thought of that.

Now they rest next to my grandfather and the bones of old hunting dogs that my dad has buried here over the years. My family knows these back prairie roads better than anyone has since the days when they were still old Métis trade routes. They believe in the country as far more than a desolate wasteland but as an unfolding promise. It holds past and future dreams and plays them out in the present. I don't want to speak to old gods but they're here. Always have been. Always will be.

Confessions

I write so much
Because I live with the old Métis mindset that I'm going to die tomorrow
Or live until I'm 103.

I don't believe that this earth will bring me back around again.

Confession:
I still don't know the difference between a noun, verb, adverb, etc.,
Or any form of grammar.

Another confession:
I want to live in matriarchy again
All my best bosses have been intimidatingly smart Cree/Dene/
    Tutchone women
Who didn't give a fuck about a white man's feelings.
I'd write poem after poem for all of them.

Last one:
I think all of this is going to come crumbling down before I'm dead
And I'm not worried about it at all.
The land knows its way around me.

The Sun's Always Shining on Saskatchewan

I wake up an hour before the dawn.
The smell of eggs frying in butter,
Split breakfast sausages, the discount kind,
Nabob in the pot.
And an old country song on the AM radio singing us the sunrise.
You're standing there, old flannel shirt tucked into loose blue jeans,
Held up by suspenders; you were always way too skinny for your
Own good. Dreaming of a future, in your wildest imagination you
Couldn't imagine living this long, having this much luxury, always
Thought you'd be dead on the prairie. Wind and porcupines gnawing
Away on your bones.
I can't imagine that in five years you'll be gone.
I'll be laid up in bed with a busted-up leg, your ashes
On the bookshelf next to a bison skull that we dug out of
The banks of the Moose Jaw River back when I was
Still scared to lose everything.
Couldn't sleep because of the spins,
Wanting nothing more than to make everyone happy.
Something I still haven't figured out,
But you never gave a shit about that.

The sun's always shining in Saskatchewan.
The sun's always shining in Saskatchewan.
The sun's always shining in Saskatchewan.
The sun's always shining on Saskatchewan.
I just want to talk to you again.

Howling Wolves

I would like to see you again
Not wrapped in the likes of Instagram posts
Thirsty dudes tapping hearts and comments
But the way we were when we were kids
Playing wolves in the back hills of Buffalo Pound
Running forever through God's Country
After who knows what and
Gorging on early August saskatoons.

We could be like
Métis gods lounged Hera-and-Zeus style
On the peak of Turtle Mountain.
Feeding each other saskatoons.
Drinking dandelion wine from
Goblets made from the skulls of
NWMP.

We could be like Métis gods
Stealing fire, a Prometheus alliance
And bringing it back to the prairie
Burn it all down.

We could be like
Métis gods watching from the backs of
Red River carts as
Zeus wrestles the Thunderbird
And the Thunderbird will always win.

Dan of the North

Once I awoke to the sounds of a .22 rifle
Chambering shorts onto the tent canvas
As my uncle plunked a couple grouse that had made their way into our camp
It's unnerving to be woken up to the sounds of bullets in the north
But when you dream in Gabriel García Márquez
Notions of one hundred years of solitude
You can see why the north still exists outside the margins of settler society
Up here the bush is still everything
And it always will be.

My uncle pan-fries the grouse in the cast iron skillets
Left from the fishing lodges
Long abandoned on islands burnt out from the fires that don't stop
I bring my heart out and set it on the pan
With the grouse breasts and let the meat
Sear up to some kind of God; I'm not sure who to pray to anymore.
I'm a .22 short
Fired from the bent barrel of an ancient peep sight unit.

I want to write poems about my ex-lovers and old friends to remember them
On the nights we met. But it never comes out right. And I don't capture
Nuances and curves and the way hands hold drinks and cigarettes. It's hard
Turning thirty when all you want to be is twenty-five forever.

Big Coyote, That One

I looked to my left and there was a pack of coyotes running alongside my 4Runner. They kept pace with their puffed-out city shine coats and muscles fuelled by the scraps of alleyways and ravines. I sped up. Not because I wanted to lose them, but because I wanted to see just how long they would run alongside me. There were four of them and the way they ran down my old SUV, you knew that these empty nocturnal city streets were their playground.

We passed a McDonald's, and two coyotes trailed off to scour the dropped drive-thru French fries, and I admit that I wanted to join them. The poker game I was coming from went long that night and I forgot to eat before going. I didn't lose any money, but I didn't make any either, which left me without emotion or feeling. When really I just craved a high or a low. A couple double cheeseburgers and fries would hit well and give me that immediate high right away and then that low the next morning. But the big coyote leading the way wanted to run, so I pressed down on the pedal and brought us up to eighty kilometres per hour. The big coyote glanced over at me and winked. Then the light turned red and I barely managed to brake in time. The pack had no problem, and they milled about the 4Runner on the otherwise-empty city street while we waited to get back to our endless cruise through the night.

Far north of us a siren started wailing as an ambulance left the university hospital. The coyotes all stopped their milling and started howling and yipping along with it. The McDonald's coyotes caught up and joined in the chorus and a few more that I hadn't seen before came out of the damp alleys to sing. I hammered on the horn a couple of times. My version of a howl, but it felt lacklustre next to the primal call and response of the pack that surrounded me so I stuck my head out the window and let go with a ooooooooooo-OOOOOOOOOOOO-ooooooooooo that might impress a pup but just got me a look of pity from the big coyote. I'm working on it, I said, but she disregarded me and the light turned green and we started our race.

She ran out in front of the 4Runner with three haunchy strong males following behind. These weren't the coyotes they show you on the city's awareness program. These were the children of extinct prairie wolves and distant relations of the grizzlies that ran behind the bison. I kept driving behind them, while the rest of the pack ran alongside and around. Where I normally would have turned off to go back to my neighbourhood the pack kept going straight and I went with them. I kept staring at the big coyote alpha female in the front. She was strong, beautiful, a touch of anger and protection rolled into a glimmer in the eye and I realized that I would do anything for her. Anything at all. I never wanted to stop our run. I never wanted to lose the fire that reflected from the moonlight off her auburn coat.

Long Days (1)

Long days. I want to move to Vancouver and swim in the ocean after the wind pushes the sewage out to the strait. Crystal water. Come back to visit I watch as you tepidly approach my new puppy because you want to make sure she falls in love with you. If a dog takes after its owner, I don't think that will be a problem.

But while I sit in winter Edmonton looking out over Papaschase IR 136 in black and white, I follow the cedar waxwings as they get drunk off the last fermented red berries still clinging to the trees. It distresses me to know that you're unhappy sitting in rooms full of stranger bros and rich kids who feel the law will be something that saves their:

Bank accounts
Relationships
Status
Parental worth
Societal worth

I want to rip apart the textbooks that cause you so much heartache. You've figured out that the system we live in was never intended to support us. You're not sure how you're going to be able to take this and flip it on its head to shake down the injustices. And I couldn't tell you anything you didn't already know. I've resigned myself to the idea that the best way forward for both of us is to do the classic millennial move and buy a cabin somewhere up the coast. With internet service. So, I can teach college courses, and you can provide legal services. But then again, we both love the action of the city, just not everything that comes with it. So, who knows.

The Big Explosion

I follow your steps, backstreet coyote
Under graffiti tagged *Land Back* and *Fuck Colonialism*
To the diner where I eat early-morning breakfasts
For $5.95 with unlimited coffee
While the first commuters drift by in River Valley fog.
I have stories of how my grandfather came here once
Lost in the throes of dementia past
He ordered the biggest pizza he could get
The man loved a good ham and pineapple. You only exist in the present.
I watch as you skulk around the trash bins,
Plumped-up winter coat looking on point
From a steady diet of the shreds of our city.
You belong here just as much as I do.
But I'd break down these buildings
And give them back to the birds if I could.

One of the last times I came here was with my brother and a swamp
biologist who was sleeping with me. Telling me sexy dreams of peat
moss, I think. Something that doesn't interest you but holds me cap-
tured in memory. Every once in a while, she still drunk texts me nice
things late at night. And I'm glad that I cross her mind. She had an owl
tattooed across her chest and a bison skull on her back. Life and death.

I follow your steps, backstreet coyote,
Past the bars I spent my twenties telling stories in.
Boarded up now to make way for commercial box stores and fancy wine.

I Dream of My Family

Do you ever dream in what-ifs?
Of grass growing on dirt fields
Graves covered in saskatoon bushes
And gardens that produce throughout
The winter.

Of a collective pushback in the 1870s

From the Cree, Blackfoot, Nakoda and Métis
Against encroaching settlers and Americans
Driving them from the prairies on the backs
Of bison.

Of grouse that dance throughout the short springs
On leks that have seen thousands of years of
Footprints trampling prairie grass down and down
Under song. Fly into the moon and bring back
The stars.

Of a future that saw us take back the notion of
Crown land and return it to those who maintain
Stewardship in a reciprocal fashion. Speak the
Words but don't hold them to your heart. Fall
From grace.

Prairie Dust

The morning when you realize home never existed
It's just in the idea of the dirt and dust
Kicked up by pickup trucks at uncontrolled prairie intersections
Where the rustiest bucket gets the right of way
And the coolest farmer barely twitches the finger on the top
Of the steering wheel to acknowledge you coming back
From cities that only work over the money that you make
From self-destruction
From selling out
From abandoning a dream
All the things that when you wake up you'll try and unsee
It gets the darkest before the dawn
That's okay
Home is when you realize that there will always be a story living on.

Long Days (II)

Long days. You finished law school, and we went out to the bar and read each other passages from the textbook that you brought with you. I sang "Californication," even though it wasn't karaoke night, to get us free Jameson shots. You dropkicked your textbook into the table next to us, and we got kicked out. A solid start to your legal career. I moved to Vancouver and didn't buy a cabin but paid a lot for rent and regretted rain and that we didn't see each other as often as we should have. I counted boats in False Creek and you served tables before heading back to live out your dream of being more Serbian, searching for something not defined within a colonial legal structure. Long overdue. I hit the road searching for some sort of bird to bring me clarity. You questioned everything.

Crows Are the Magpies of 2022

Magpie poetry ended the moment I got bombarded by Burnaby crows
Picking mussels at low tide and dropping them on Seawall tourists
Which is really what we all are. They scatter under shells and avoid the
Shit from a thousand crows circling, cawing, posting up outside the police
Yards under the Cambie Bridge to keep an eye on those who impose
False justice when a crow court is all that was ever needed to keep some
Semblance of order on this land. Towing lower middle-class income lines.
Always on the brink of owing someone everything.
When a crow owes nothing more than a couple
Shells to sprinkle down on concrete.

I try to find myself within their song but it doesn't echo home as we both know
That I'm just a passing visitor on this land. Invited guest but it doesn't make a
Difference because I'm outside of my element of flat open spaces. I want a boat
But I'll satisfy myself with looking out at the False Creek wreckages and wonder
What stories they've all seen.
What stories and worlds do the crows see on their
Sunrise and sunset migrations back to Burnaby.
The ultimate commuter. I'm displaced but not out of order.
I can take a big wooden spoon and stir up False Creek
To kick up the leftovers and the shells
That the crows can't reach. So they know that
I'm paying tribute. Are crows native to here? Our crows native to hear?

Whoever thought it was a good idea to sell my truck was mistaken.
Whoever thought it was a good idea to try to impose colonial governance
On all these territories stretching far across this land was mistaken.
It'll come back on them.

Just like these fucking crows come back every day.

Mental Health

A friend gifts me a relaxation bath bomb
Because my mind is a thousand eggs.

I shatter myself on sidewalks
Break empty into the cracks
Stomped down, again and again.

Stay alive for dogs and fall leaves
Shotguns singing in September wind.

A line of pimples forms on the back of my neck
Reminding me of the hours I sit lonesome in
The tub, trying not to drown this time.

I want to walk forever. Just not where people fight.
My head can't take that anymore.

Forget about the other half I buried in a snow fort
In a Moose Jaw elementary school field. When I
Took off my jacket and threw it to the wind. Trying
To make a friend. All I ever wanted was to be held
Again.

Spend days with tears wrapped around my throat, gripping
That shit box tighter and tighter. Force out the garbage of a
Dream left spent drowning in a culvert.

I'm pulled in by night
Bodies strung up on barbed-wire fences on a back highway in
Southern Saskatchewan. I still hear the crying of the little girl
I wrapped in a blanket and brought back to my truck so she
Wouldn't have to spend another minute next to the dead.
Fifteen years later I wonder where she ended up.
She'd be in her mid-twenties now.
I left when the ambulance showed.

Pick my nose until it bleeds
Eat until I puke
Fuck until I'm fucked.

I want someone to yell at me. Take me to the principal's office.
Beat the shit out of me. I want to feel something
Other than drowning.

Worth It

Set aside the pen for golf clubs for a bit,
Dog-training whistles, leashes and comic books.
Pen is probably not the write word to use,
Since I type everything on a shitty iPad
Keyboard. Mainly in the bathtub.
My spot of isolation and thought in the
Morning before sitting down to go through the
Administrative processes of trying to make
A college not suck for Indigenous people.

I watched from under the chlorine water as you dove
Into pools from the three-metre board while the sun
Shone fireworks above you.
How you would pretend that you were going to
Bellyflop so the crowd at the outdoor pool would gasp.
The ultimate performer right to the end when you tuck
Into a dive, break the water with your hands, and pull
In tight.

I would love to microdose mushrooms with you again and
Watch the stars from the mountains. Take that 85,000-lumen
Spotlight you grabbed from god knows where and shine
Boomerangs behind shooting stars. Point out our favourites.

Then in December, you bought the star on some chintzy-ass
Website that sent you a framed certificate which you gave me
When I turned thirty. I would love it if that deed were to hold up in the year
2350 or something. Though I doubt we'll ever get there at our
Current rate.
Fuck it. Still worth it.

Bird's-Eye View

Patchwork prairie benefited by a fall from grace
I'm searching for seeds from 35,000 feet
Trying to trace old trade routes with my finger on
The glass.

I count the towns, try to find landmarks, flying everywhere
But where I should be going. There are no gods in
The clouds that you want to see and I miss a
Summer thunderstorm.

Just as much as I hope you miss me.

Just Passing Through

La Montagne Tortue ka-itohtanan
En charette kawitapasonan
Les souliers moux kakiskenan
L'ecorce de boulot kamisahonan[1]

---

1   Gabriel Dumont Institute. "La Montagne Tortue." *Gabriel Dumont Institute of Native Studies and Applied Research*, Gabriel Dumont Institute, 1996, http://www.metismuseum.ca/resource.php/07074. Accessed 11 January 2021.

Edmonton to Vancouver
We cracked pack after pack of menthol Halls
Let each one's medical sugar
Take us another twenty kilometres closer to Vancouver
Both trying not to smoke any more cigarettes
And minimize the coffee intake
To keep from having to pull over to pee.

I'm looking for yellow lines through
Snow-splooge-stained, cracked windshield
To keep from drifting into the other lane and bringing me back
To a trucker's end of route.

The old Toyota, cool 500,000 kilometres of beat-up Treaty 6 backroads
ago. Now it just exists to contain its cargo. Two middle-aged *we're not
young anymore* Métis, two Labradors and the possibility that a new
city will give us something to hold on to besides anger.

Despite its age the 4Runner doesn't like to move slower than 120
A testament contained to the constant mobility of
My ancestors who would have
Loved to have bombarded over prayerie grass
With shocks and struts instead of
Squeaky old, old, old carts that bounced a butt back to the Red River.

Although I don't think any of our ancestors made it to Vancouver, they
definitely went to Last Mountain Lake, suntanned on the shores of the
great Saskatchewan River.

The first time I saw a mountain I was thirteen years old. Straight out of Buffalo Pound and the southern prayerie where the biggest mountain was Blackstrap Ski Hill south of Saskatoon *old garbage dump with a chairlift* I couldn't keep my head inside the vehicle as we drove west from Calgary. And I tried to see the peaks of everything, to be on the top with the whole white world below my feet.

Mountains don't make sense to a prayerie child.

Now they pass in a blur as I long to get off this fucking road. How do Métis survive in cities? I want to throw every computer into the ocean and stampede back up a mountain to jump off. Spread wings and fall back to the highway followed by a faded rainbow arc of missed promises and the chances that I had to be happy.

We're going to Turtle Mountain
We're going in a Red River cart
We're going to wear moccasins
We'll wipe our asses with birchbark[2]

2   *La Montagne Tortue,* Translated by Elder Delores Cardinal of Goodfish Lake
in the NorQuest College Indigenous Student Centre. October 2019.

Edmonton to Saskatoon
Most travelled stretch,

Barely seventeen I fell asleep outside of Maidstone and the rumble strips jarred me awake with a shot of adrenaline that kept my eyes glued to the most hetero highway that exists. So fucking straight. And I was going to meet my MSN Messenger crush that I spent all night chatting with. Changing statuses so she could see my infatuated hints through shitty song lyrics. That all seemed so important. I don't remember what we talked about.

We fuck with the enthusiasm of teenagers in the back seat of my grandparents' minivan *that I'm borrowing for(ever) the summer* in every highway rest stop along the way. We drink bellinis with our fake IDs at the Moxies in the parking lot of a bookstore. Purchased with the tips you get from greasy old men at the restaurant back in Edmonton. Get drunk. Get back at it. The only thing we eat is each other for a week.

During the day we hide among the bookstore shelves. I read you old white Jewish Montreal poetry. And you pretend to be interested, until your hand slips inside my jeans. When I'm about to finish you pull it out and I cum all over the pages of the *Norton Anthology of English Literature*.

All it brought was conviction of promise and a future that turned out infinitely better than what we conceived together,
A couple Métis born into prayerie poverty.

My cousin dreams in old travelling songs
He sings them between his snores
Wrapped up with a sleeping bag pulled
Tight over his head.

My cousin dreams that we're paddling
Here from Montreal. Shaking hands with
Our ancestors who signed Treaty 6
And then faded back into the night.

My cousin dreams of dishes of canned
Saskatoon berries, smoked jackfish,
Dried moosemeat and fried bread.
We eat together forever.

On the Visiting Trail

Spending summers on the never-ending visiting tour of my grand-parents in their ill-conceived homemade camper perched precariously on top of a tiny quarter-ton truck. We sat in the camper and played hand after hand of crib while my grandfather drove us from relation to relation. The way my grandmother's hand looked as it stretched through the window on the back of the truck cab to pass him a coffee or tea as hour after hour flew by on old lands. Old from before I was born. Speak of history and they'll tell you that this isn't a new highway. It's been here forever and will exist long after the concrete crumbles back into land.

My grandfather finds parfleche bags holding lost balls of pemmican along the old highways. Bison leather crumbles to dust under the constant movement of soil. You can still see chokecherry pits ground into the petrified, pounded meat. The blades of farm equipment lobbed off grouse wings and settled them into the constant combine dust of the fall. A true Saskatchewan sunset is obscured. Nothing was supposed to grow here. It's country that's better left to the sharptails and all the generations who didn't think of land as money and profit but as an extension of our hearts.

Barely thirty-two I don't understand why I can't settle down. The need for constant mobility has me dreaming of being back on the road counting the ravens that crowd the carcasses, tossed like they didn't mean anything into the ditches. They fly circles of roadkill into the sky and drop bullets back to earth. Better off on wings, I don't know if I can ever fly far enough to escape the reach of a prayerie childhood. Pick saskatoon berries from the hills of the Qu'Appelle Valley. Bison bones from the waters of Buffalo Pound. My father found arrowheads and old tipi circles in every Greyhound bus he ever rode.

We're on the prayerie
We're on the prayerie
We're on the prayerie
We're on the prayerie[3]

---

3   My five-year-old self singing to my parents or grandparents every time we
    went anywhere.

Drayton Valley to Edmonton

Undergrad poetry about blue Nomex coveralls caked in sucker-rod grease. Stripping down in a hotshot truck parked outside of the humanities building. Blending up truck-stop coffee, cigarettes, sweat, cheap beer, and McDonald's fries and then snorting it on the back of a textbook on the history of the Canadian plains. I don't want to drive in circles but then I don't know how else to survive.

Paying tabs at the campus bars with twenties caked in oil sludge. I know this highway better drunk than I do sober. And old truckers tell me that I'm going to crash. It's just a matter of time. I look for the remains of my last years of innocence in the ditches. Watch shows on a laptop propped up on the dash to kill the kilometres of boredom. You can only drive a road so often.

My father brings us to Asian restaurants on the outskirts of the Papaschase Industrial Park. Travel confined to a buffet, cashew chicken and cheap *but so good* bowls of spicy noodles. It's not much. But it helps to teach a small-town Métis kid that there is more world outside of a pumpjack in a schoolyard. Driving back on snow-packed roads he dodges wayward semis in a white Dodge Caravan. Asks if anyone wants to listen to the cassette audiobook of *Moby Dick*.

The road glistens with sweat from every job I failed to perform at until put on a pedestal to ANNOUNCE my heritage and family stories for the validation of white institutions. Am I NDN enough for you? For you to listen to me? Or should I get back behind that fucking wheel and drive until the moose stands up in front of the sunset and tells me that home isn't in a building, but in the landscapes that cradled me next to their breasts.

Granny's hands, stained purple
Placing beads on her ancestors' needles
Candlelit nights.
She sews moosehide into moccasins
To sell to white men for their wives.

Buffalo Pound to Saskatoon
Years ago I listed naked under patchwork quilts
The different towns driven through
Between Buffalo Pound and Saskatoon
Just the sort of sexy pillow talk that every woman dreams of.
And we talked about one day
Going to Buffalo Pound to see if any of the old
Cabins were still around. Burnt down.

Outside of Craik my grandfather asks me
To lean out the passenger-side window
And feel if that's a crack or a bug. We massacre en masse on the grid
roads. Long before double lanes. I wanted every excuse to spend all day
with him looking for the faint fog breath of mule deer in the Qu'Appelle
Valley ridges. Sit on the tailgate of the truck and drink root beer while
he drank pints in the small-town pubs. I didn't want to see him die, even
though he dreamt of moose steaks and called out to them, grunting
with his last breath.

If you ever took a Greyhound.
The move was two shots of cheap whisky and a pint.
Shoot the first, dump the second all over you and chug the beer.
Make sure you're first in line. Get the back bench.
Lay down.
Coat over head.
No one will bother you.

Eight winters, riding the bus from Saskatoon to Moose Jaw.
The bartender wouldn't serve me.
And no one wants to be on a stinking milk run.

I want to dream of the sunset when I was seventeen
When cigarettes still tasted like flying.

Edmonton to Lethbridge
Combine dust tilts the sunrise upside down
I'd bust up each one of these machines with an old Sherwood hockey stick
To bring back grouse and plains grizzlies.

My septum destroyed from working harvests
Spending time in the seed-cleaning plant with an older friend
Who kept me from blowing up behind a rink
Like a frostbitten tree. In the exploding moon.
Hypothermia is always present in a drunkard.

My girlfriend buys me a bus ticket to see her in Beaver Hills
I only have enough change for a Junior Chicken or a bag of
Doritos. I lick the cheese dust off of my fingers and wonder
Who the fuck can afford beef jerky.

Chinook winds make a campus smell like rat farts. Or
More accurately cow disease.
Prayeries didn't used to smell like death.
I'd take bison musk over this any day.

I live inside the mosquito din
Surrounded by dancing sharptail grouse
Each one an infinite lek unto itself
I am the rolling hills
Prayerie potholes
The lonesome A&W billboard G R DERS GO!

I live inside the discarded Pilsner can
Waiting alongside the purple roots of sweetgrass.
I grow into the soiled earth and watch
The world go by
One truck at a time.

Drayton Valley to Everywhere in Central Alberta
Played hockey with guys who would list out women they'd slept with
Counted trophies,
When they got fat they switched to animals.
Counted trophies,
Same dudes who would be pissing on each other in the showers
Swinging naked cocks in hand from the weird randomly placed
Metal bars.
We'd put on helmets and gloves and beat the shit out of each other
Tilting. Knockin' skulls.
Broken bones and concussions and parent fights
I wondered why my dad (and the other Native parents) always sat
On the other side of the rink from the whites.

Why we went to a different restaurant than the rest of the team.
Why we carpooled together and not with the others.

I don't like math. I don't like counting.

I pick out faces in the news articles about white supremacists.
Think I ran that fuck into a crossbar back in the day.

I drove an old truck loaded with stolen fireworks to a house party
Shot them off everywhere in the city and tried to drive away before
The cops came. But I locked my keys in the truck.

I would have driven right off the High Level and let the eagles
Pick me and carve me up.
Scatter my bones among the bros.

Elbows, knees, backs arched on a buffalo rug
In front of the birch-burning fire
The fur bristles against our bare skin
I grasp onto your hip bones
When I cum you bury your face
Deep inside
To breathe
Leftover smoke
Tanned hide.

Papaschase IR 136 to Moose Jaw to Calgary
I rise up and drain my lavender-infused
Bathwater back to the Mill Creek
Past the shanties of my granny. Talk beautiful stories of woodpecker
Prosperity. Place pennies on railroad tracks
And watch as the cars tumble up
Into the sky and onto the backs
Of thousands of sage grouse who returned
For one last dance among the stars on the niskak highway.

They bring the railcars to Calgary.
Bitumen blackens the sky and fills the corporate
Headquarters with unrefined crude.
Arcteryx-laden hikers climb mountains
Use prayer flags as trail markers in an attempt to conquer everything.

So many songs. I'll hold my fiddle high in the air
And play out a keeping time

Reel to bring back the Red River carts from the Dakotas. Stomp spoons
and let the dogs howl. We're needed in the north. I can take the tip of
the nose off of a moose from three hundred yards with an open site,
bent barrel, 30-30.

Dumont sir, I'm at your service.

My first trapline
Is on the docks of Buffalo Pound.
Drop bricks tied to a frayed yellow rope
into the water.

I pull in the trap as fast as my five-year-old
Muscles will let me,
So the crayfish can't swim backwards out of
The holes in the bricks.

Let it go.
Let it go.
You're just passing through.

II.
MÉTIS MAGIC

Who the Fuck Stole My Catalytic Converter?

I'm a foregone conclusion
Wrapped up malevolence in a fabricated smile
Screaming inside while laughing and speaking the language
Of bureaucracy mimicked from years of listening to vague promises.

I'm a tipped-over shopping cart
Outside your storefront window, possessions and ancestry laid
Naked, bare, for academic analysis and research into failure of
Genetics to turn me the colour you wish to see in professional development.

I'm a catalytic converter
Hacked off on thunderstorm nights under quarter-moon skies.
Making cash for diversity and inclusion. Numbers are just a scrapyard
Shoved full of precious metals to be sold off to the highest bidder.

I'm a lukewarm coffee cup
Sitting beside a steaming bathtub, spilled across white porcelain.
To be lapped up by the rising waves of a back eddy's whirlpool,
Sucking down and down and down and down and down.

cihcicâpânâskos

Late-night Instagram group calls and whispered threats of tearing down systems while screeching tires burn holes in virtual smoke-show screens. We spin laps in anticipation of being together in comfortable silence. Tending to controllers like gardens. Back-alley raspberries sustain the constant drifting. I'm reduced to the friendship of speakerphones and the idea that there is a person behind imagery and voice, feeling something, anything. Because I'm really not. I'd bring our tracks into the bush of the swampy Beaver Hills muskeg and let the bison rise up from their graves beneath bogs. Kart racing is in my blood; I didn't understand it would be reduced to a video game. But I love the way that voices sound, hidden against the loneliness of the night.

And on the Fourth Day, God Created ...

A creation story is an empty radio bingo card, an unpegged crib board, a crisp crokinole table. Just holding enough hope within the potential for future.

My creation story is birthed into a canoe, hidden from the summer's dry heat in the shade of a back bay under old ochre-stained rocks. An altar to gods that don't believe in that sort of thing.

My creation story is a morning bath after a sunrise run. Fucking strong coffee and lavender salts and the hope for a day that believes in the beauty of language and dreams.

My creation story is a Labrador retriever barrelling under caragana rows after coveys of grouse and pheasants. That same dog snuggled up on my feet as I sang sorrow songs.

A creation story is just that. Something to hold on to when the darkness comes in fast and there isn't hope in artificial light. At least until willow buds pop.

Another Day in Treaty 6

Magpies build back-alley nests under trapper eyes
Set off snares in brush laid bare
Tan hides.

I'm a star plucker. Reaching high high high high
Every night in my four a.m. dog-snore dreams
Just survive.

My aunties throw perogies and bannock at each other
Across community hall tabletops
Treaty days.

Porcupines chew up tops of bush trees carving their
Initials into wood like high school kids
Land back.

I'm dragging out my stencils and spray-painting
QUIT YOUR JOB like it's 2009 again
Scared kid.

My friends enter through apartment windows
Our own little oasis behind a baseball bat
Drink up.

I'm trying to turn myself into an elephant again
The old avenue uncle taps into the pub
Sings loud.

Skunks mating on my front yard spray me down
Five-thirty a.m. and I'm a kid again running
Buffalo Pound.

My grandfather likes to cheat at cards, slips an ace
Up his sleeve that doesn't quite make it
Dementia grasp.

I'm crying on the number 9 northside bus
Coming down over empty city blocks
Stay home.

iskwesisihkân

How much weight can you put in the three cereals of my childhood
Shredded wheat
Puffed wheat
And on special occasions, Mini-Wheats.
Our household a Saskatchewan flag
Advertisement for prairie prosperity
The dream never played out for us
Or any of the other families that sat
Down to bowls of wheat because that's
What they told us to do.

How much weight can you put in the sugar-laden cereals my
Grandparents shovelled into all of my cousins' and my mouths
While we sat under tobacco-stained walls and champagne-cork
Ceilings. Where so many dollars had changed hands on late-
Night card tricks. Every time I play late-night cards I think of my
Grandfather skipping out of work to get on a poker hot streak
That equalled his military earnings for a year. Sneak back the
Fucking land in whatever way you can. He wandered into a
Recruiting office in the late 40s in Regina, Saskatchewan after
One night in a bar and that decision defined our family's existence.

My grandmother joined up to escape the constant badgering of her
Family to get married. Because, you know, she was twenty-four and
There was always another bachelor waiting back at her parents'
Road-allowance shack north of St. Paul whenever she returned
Home from the city. Where she, oh she partied, and she loved to
Party and still does. This is where I get that from.

Then in fucking Ottawa of all places they met up.
Under the statues' colonial gaze on the people who
Decided that they were properly assimilated now.
Good ol' Métis joining the military, get some.
Service to the nation. They'd rather serve the
Statues their fucking heads on a platter. But they
Did that through stealing every little thing they
Could. Smuggled out of the bases in the trash
Cushions loaded up with anything they could get.
They told me that magpies shit on the statues.
Why wouldn't they?

An Ode to Graduate Studies

The end result of an MFA is the idea that writing is fucking stupid,
Everyone sees it differently. But you do it anyway because, hell,
What do you have to lose? I don't see the veins of poems the way
My friends do. I just blab on and on about nothing in particular, a
Skill set for the small talk that isn't available in a workshop but can
Be sweated out at the bar. I'm a conversation, a first-date icebreaker,
A scared thirty-something white-coded Métis poet trying to keep up with
Turning language and thought into something discepherable (spelled that
Shit wrong) for others' enjoyment. I don't have an audience except the
Early-morning birds, skunks, porcupines, coyotes and Labrador retrievers
That greet the sunrise with me every morning. Waniska motherfuckers.

Finding Scrip

I Google map the locations of scrip allotments
That were never settled.
Wonder if anyone would object to me setting
Up in the wall tent.
Just for a visit, you know. Maybe through the
Berrypicking season.
I dump canned Saskatoon berry juice into carbonated
Water. What the fuck
Would my ancestors think about that move?

I hear crib table giggles as my grandparents
Take their friends to
Skunk city. Above the table cigarette smoke swirls,
Stained walls and dents
From a thousand champagne corks they let buck
For any occasion at all.
My grandfather sets up a canvas tent they call
The casino and family
Gathers under it to bet away their earnings from
The fall guiding season.

Wishing on a Walleye

I flick a hockey-bro lighter and read your texts
About the nuances of Elder story
Put said lighter to sage. Sit in smoke.
Start peeling the label back to expose its
White beginnings and wonder what party I stole this from back in the day.

You run circles on old fur-trade stomping grounds
To bring warmth back into body
I like to think you're just imprinting more
Footsteps on the land so the ancestors know
That you've returned home. Your own call-out to their story.
Love radiates through
The land.

I'll take my shirt off, sit and smoke at the top
Of the stairs that run up from pehonan.
Make the bros and broettes dodge my flabby bod
As I soak in birdsong. Until
You decide to kick my ass for taking too long
In delivering moosemeat and a common
Understanding that working for bureaucracy sucks moose nuts.

I'm continually dumbfounded by the way you can
Write history in the sky. Paint water through veins.
Touch life back into concrete. Troll wannabe politicians on Twitter.
I want to

Be a bison herd with the strength to tear hooves
Through concrete and give you back all
The downtown parking lots.

I wish we only spoke in nehiyawewin.
I wish we never looked at the northern lights.
I wish we could ride on crane wings on the thermals of the city.
I wish we could bring back all the kids who never had a chance.
I wish that the Oilers won the cup and then they
Turned the arena into the Papaschase Reserve.
I wish they gave all that 50/50 money back to the people
Whose land they're playing hockey on.

But I'll settle for kicking your ass in Mario Kart on the nightly.

Métis Magic

I'm the three a.m. magician,
Cutting cards for drunk eyes
Claiming hearts are diamonds
And that this old apartment
Doesn't hurl up veiled sweat
From thousands of lost hands.

I'm the three a.m. magician,
Throwing decks of suits into
The fire. Late-night pizza orders
And homebrew-fuelled forty-
Dollar hands, slide that ace out
Of the sleeve. Take it down.

I'm the three a.m. magician,
Constant entertainment hide-and-seek
After the last call in a bachelor suite.
Disappear under the sheets into our
Jameson-fuelled lust. Knowing the end-
Game is three weeks from now.

I'm the three a.m. magician,
Waking up to hide snow goose decoys
Across frozen prairie. While the world
Sleeps the northern lights dance down
Like a snow goose knuckleballing into
the blinds. Paint the sky in your tundra.

I'm the three a.m. magician,
Following buffalo herds south into the
Dakotas. Tapping out the rhythms to
The sound of horses' heartbeats while
Chasing them back from the dead. Scattering
Ashes, on top of sleeping rocky giants.

Pandemic Coping Mechanisms

Follow your eighteen-year-old dreams of quitting jobs
Play late-night poker until the cash runs out
Switch to video games and tattoos
Addiction runs deep, so stay away from the booze.

Nightly weed gummies, roll forty doobies at once and
Puff back for a couple weeks. Get puppy, train puppy,
Love puppy, think about moving west because Alberta
Is the place where dreams go to die.

Unless they give back the land and we can live under the
Guidance of matriarchs and not political games. I want to
See the mountains remain intact. The birds come back. The
Caribou and moose expand forever.

A pandemic love song is: Just survive.

Buffalo Pound

Changing winds
It was never supposed to snow this much
Makes a prairie boy
Feel at home
Sitting on a bench
Drinking black coffee
Staring out at rich people's
Yachts. Dreaming of the
Twelve-foot aluminum boat
With the 9.9 Merc
That raced across
Buffalo Pound
To the causeway
Where prairie boys
Jump into the
Water.

Meatball Subs

I'm the kind of guy who orders a meatball sub on a first date.
Who dreams in constellations and northern lights.
I'm a whisper. A woodpecker's tap.
I'll smile circles. Try to give it all back.

III.
OLD GODS

Camping

Break dawn with iyinisip wings whistling through crisp darkness,
The first visitors on an egg-crack-horizon sunrise.
Fall light is yolk hitting a cast iron pan,
On the wood stove burning birch in the old canvas tent.

A kettle filled with muskeg tea simmers through the seasons,
Topped up with first snow. Under northern lights
The dogs howl back at coyote wails.
And the ghosts of all those who will stand witness to a new day
Join them in their song.

Forgotten Gravesites

When I was in my early twenties, I would drink myself into oblivion and walk across the old green Walterdale Bridge throwing glass Pilsner bottles into the air and wondering just how deep the river was beneath my feet. My grandmother told me of her brother, who jumped from the High Level Bridge but was picked up by Eagles and carried away to the bush of their youth, north of St-Paul-des-Métis. I thought that maybe an old namew would rise up out of the swift-moving waters and swallow me whole and carry me in its stomach like red ochre dye back to Montreal. I'd like to speak terrible French with beautiful people while the stars and songs of ancestors ring out, bellow out from the Plateau.

I'd howl into the Papaschase gravestones speaking shattered Cree; the only word I knew was love, and how badly I wanted someone to love me. Sit beside my relatives' gravestones, light a cigarette, wish I could afford more booze. Try to pinpoint the house that Frank Oliver lives in. He owes me and my family and my friends and my friends' families and our relations lots of money. But I'll take it back in Land.

We can release bison throughout the River Valley again and see modern agriculture trampled into prairie grasses. I know the money families are still kicking around. Basking in champagne-filled hot tubs and reading each other copies of the Indian Act as a form of comedy.

You can only spend so much time trying to be something you're not. I wanted to be rich and elevate above the poverty of my life. To hit another stride of living and join in on old-money worlds. But I'm fucking Métis born in the dying throes of fur-trade paradise and taking refuge under stampeding bison. I find my solace in blood dripping through the bones buried long ago.

Shatter earth. Shatter my aspiration.

I didn't want to believe in a river. But what else does one have for gods? I can't believe in money. I tried that and it didn't work. Time is a social construct and it fucks me daily.

I think of how nice it feels to have the cool old graveyard grass, manicured Kentucky blue or some bullshit like that, on my head. A baptism of sorts I guess.

I want to shoot a shotgun up in the air and feel the pellets fall back to the 1880s and smash through the skulls of the fuckers who burned down my great-grandmother's house on the south side of the river. They said, repent in the flames, and I too can achieve the benefit of my kinscape, money, and develop a passion for flittering things.

But I don't.

I believe in stories of grandmothers and aunties, and the flowing forever lights from the wall tents in the Mill Creek Ravine.

Memory

Under what sky
Did you think
We could reach
For our grandmother's
Hands and pull
Beaded flowers
From fingertips
Hardened by
Needlepoint?

And when did
You think that
We could taste
And smell
Rat root boiled
Into tea,
Bear grease
Rubbed on
Vertigo minds?

Mill Creek

Drink slaughterhouse water from the old creek
Burn down coyote laughter
Howling in the hills
Bite the porcupine's back
Turn graves into an off-leash dog park
Watch the plastic build up next to the bones
Discard pig carcasses
Drag the creek

Turn it all into an industrial park stomping ground
For the warehouses and factories that outlet into a
Storm sewer mixed with chemical refuse.

The remains of the shanties and fiddles busted up
And carried off by the rising red water.
Chemical mix of walleye scales and memories.
Man-made waterfalls on top banks spewing out the
Excrement of money all over the side of the city.

Investments

I'm angry on the page because I don't know how to turn off a smile.
Throw my ancestry on a blackboard for your dissection,
I don't mind sharing with those
Who are looking to see a snagging history.
Standing naked in front of the classroom waiting for a final judgment.
Some god on a throne of white authenticity.
Justify my existence one birth at a time.
I asked my granny why none of her aunties or uncles
Had those little lines sticking down.
They died from the flu.
That meant something different back then.

Granny worries about moonshine and the Toronto Blue Jays.
She doesn't give a shit what critics have to say about her.
Does the classic deferral to authority and talks smack
Behind their backs.
Makes straight cash from playing cards into the long nights
In the basement of the Legion.
Doesn't believe in the future, saves money in a coffee tin
In the back of the fridge.
Invests in blackberries and saskatoons.
Believes in kinship, but only the bush kind.

Cook County Cowboys and the Land They Two-Step On

Under western skies,
Faux cowboys in beaded bolo ties
Trade barbs over IPAs at a downtown pub
Never been on a horse, never been in the suck.

Judgment comes from a woodpecker's early morning taps
Magpies spread treasures through the old reserve
Bury story. Bury memory. Bury it deep, fucker.
Because if they ever dig it up again it's coming in hot.

Heart belongs strung up on the front of a canvas tent like a pair
Of old bull antlers. Bison skulls crawl out of River Valley banks
Floods bring back the dead and all their dreams. It's hard to think
Of 1888 and what a future meant, when everything is a screen.

The God of Willow and Muskeg

Early light, purple dregs of a failed sunrise, watch cattail shadows,
put my hands around my grandfather's old lever-action Savage,
raise the open sites up to the god of willow and muskeg.
Sing them their honour song.
Squeeze the trigger.

My brother dreams of butchering moose,
Blood-stained cheap blue tarps and the knife edge moving through
      the cold flesh.
That slowly freezes your hands.
We're four days into the fall harvest.
Turned on by a propane heater's loud warmth.
I hold my frozen hands next to the penetrating heat,
Let life come back into my blood while my brother
Sharpens his knife. Again. And we crack the door in
The old trap shed to let the oxygen back in. Again.
Carbon monoxide detector's been barking but we took the batteries out.
While the moose, quartered before our five-
K pack-out through the heavy bush, sits on brown butcher paper.
Each quarter strung up on a cross,
Hanging for our sins.

I dropped a green and gold glove, a gift from a professor at
The university for a lecture on Métis history.
A class I failed under a different idol.
Swag for culture. Somewhere on the trail.
I hope it keeps the coyote's paws warm.

Next to the god of willow and muskeg

Each packet of meat I wrap in butcher paper and place into
Old yellow No Frills plastic bags.

Ten pounds of ground, stew and steaks
For my cousin who can't leave the city.

The same for my friend who writes beautiful poetry
And doesn't leave her studio apartment.

The nose, tongue, steaks and tenderloin
For the Elder who lives in the Medicine Hills.

Fifty pounds of stew, steaks, ground and sausages
The hide, summer culture camp bound.
For my friend's auntie out on the Rez with so many kids
Who call her kohkom and lift her high up in their perfect
Hearts as she dishes out the hamburger soup that makes
All of us sing our own honour song. She wraps us all
In her cooking and lets us sit beside her fire while she
Tells us, with nothing more than the filling of a bowl,
That we'll always have a home.

Wednesday Wing Night

Magpies always know when it's wing night.
They follow the throngs from pub to pub
Turn into middle-aged men with harmless eyes.
Sit at tables and order thirty-five-cent chemical
Chicken and reminisce about the glory days
Of ten-cent wings and stomachs that could
Turn hot sauce into purple iridescence.

Magpies line their human pockets with bones
Discreetly under belly folds and armpits, shoved
Into a body's crevices. To scatter across the alleys
And backyards under northern skies.
A tribute to frozen feathers and long
Dark nights. Magpies know that old gods watch for
Those who move within rituals.

Memories of Birds

Outside nohkum's apartment building
Three Hungarian partridge dance
Illuminated by green traffic light against
The gravel and salt and mud-encrusted
Snow.

My grandfather watches them through
His bedroom window. Memories of a
Prairie childhood watching deer and birds
Move outside the old one-room shack's
Walls.

His head, clouded in dust from no longer
Being allowed to roam the haunted hills.
Frozen lakes. Snowdrift prairie. Caragana
Rows outside an old farmyard. Remembers
Feathers.

Moving through the cold winds. He lifts
Himself up and forgets why he went into
The kitchen and can't remember that it's
Not the 1930s. He cracks a can of Pilsner,
Drinks.

Sets it back on the fridge shelf next to a
Garlic sausage and a pack of no name
Cheese slices. He pulls out the coffee tin
Where nohkum hides soniyaw. He counts it
All.

Outside the midnight partridge dance under
Red spotlights on their stage of stained snow.

Urban Hunter

Follow tracks through back sections thinking about antlers and cabins and a freezer full of moosemeat. The shit that's important. I watch my friend walk patiently and I think about his steps and the way he moves across the land in a deliberate way, while I crash and burn through bush chasing after imaginary birds and the possibility of a moose. I try to slow down to keep pace but it doesn't work and I find myself sprinting through knee-deep snow on the trail of a bull that's now running toward a Medicine Line fence. If we cross it we'll be the ones who are shot.

I smash my leg up on a ski hill being an idiot. And the Elder tells me as he lifts the pipe inside my house that it's a sign to slow down and stop this constant, incessant burnout. The go go go go. Sometimes as I sit by late-night fires I remember him and my friends sitting in a circle on the dining room floor under bison skulls. I can't go on the ground, my leg burnt out, the house is a smoke memory of NDNs moving through ceremony. She doesn't ask what happened. Just lets me fade into dust, settled on the remains of ancestors' laughter.

When everything goes away I'll sing travelling songs at the top of my lungs in a downtown neighbourhood. Awaken the magpies and blue jays who join in my call, we chase the crows out of the old staked out reserve grounds. Drum my heartbeat out on green dumpsters. Build up the old camping grounds around the fort-turned-marble-legislature. Bathe in the fountains. Spray-paint syllabics on this fucked-up governance. Watch the coyotes crawl out of the River Valley and turn back to wolves on the steps of Oliver's failure to get rid of us. Bite back.

Winter Songs

Two coyotes. Full winter coats puffed out. Follow their morning run through the back alleys and train tracks under generations of graffiti and abandoned murals of 80s sports stars. The discarded shells of burned-out and abandoned land-value-only buildings stand watch over their paw prints left in snow not yet spoiled. Somewhere above, magpies announce their arrival into the territory. Angels welcoming gods of a city gone back to the land through trumpet fare, and the remnants of an "O Canada" anthem playing on endless repeat from abandoned stadiums.

Two coyotes walk back 150 years to a time before skyscrapers and suburbs—man-made lakes, dams, bridges and power plants—and dig up the bones of ancestors laid along the riverbanks. Watch them rise up to dismantle the structures placed on top of quarter sections that divided a country. They spool back barbed wire and let the bison pound the houses into kindling for their winter fires. Marble legislature pillars crushed under the weight of an elk skull. A coyote's god lives in bones.

The North Sask

Blood is a river
That can't be damned even if all the money in the world is thrown
    into concrete
Decomposed corpses on the banks
Last year's wolf harvest

Blood is a blizzard's snow
Burying cars in snowdrifts along prairie highways
Where the road never stops
Following old nohkum cars

Blood is a falling magpie
Tracing arcs with iridescent feathers like fingers along backs
Captured in memory, routes of spiralling kin
Taking back the space above overturned trash cans

Blood is a lukewarm bath
That lost the will to heat years ago
Where dreams of alleyway raspberry bushes
Fill the water with seeds

Skunk City

Morning runs through ravines
Greeted by sikak around the curves of manifested parks over polluted
    pig factories
He lives, big boar, in the hillside of rusted-out iron bones and creosote
    boards
Under bridges, dodge needles and playing cards
But only the king of hearts

Sprayed down by skunks along backside ravine underpasses
And culverts that lead to a different time. Walk through
And it's 1885 and the woodpeckers are dancing along the poplar trees,
Tapping out a rhythm for those who travel underneath,
And late at night bust out fiddles to sing woodpecker songs too.
Paint birds in the sky with words and paint sikak in the bush with the land.

Those Birds That Hit Your Window

Cedar waxwings are the drunken spring poets
Minstrels of backyards, alleys and the shanty
Towns in the parks and ravines. They call out
To everyone to drown themselves in berries and
Pleasure, Greek-god style on the prairies. But
Don't cross a river. My car is covered in their berry
Pickings, the discarded bottles of a thousand friends
Circling frenzied and smashing into windows in a
Haze of feathers all for the pleasure of song and
Scrambling flight along the old reservation's trees
And shrubbery, transplanted from another time
When this was good white country before the NDNs
Moved back to reclaim their place, starting with my
Auntie who took flight from dying homes and brought
Her song to the friends, a sorrowful, mourning song
Carried forward on waxwing beaks. I believe in
The heartbeats of birds that don't want to stop for
Anything.

Old Gods

Lord, it's me, Conor.
You know I'm about as anti-religious as it gets.
And I haven't seriously considered a Christian god since I was twelve at
    the inner-city (Native) bible camp outside of Regina.
Or the time I tried to impress a woman by knowing weird biblical facts.
You can imagine how well that went over.

But really I just wanted to say that you should get the fuck out of Dodge,
Your days on kitaskinaw are numbered. Have been for a long time now.
The old ones are coming back strong. They never left. Just bided their time.

And I can see them now in the whirlwinds that kick up on old northern lakes.
And I can see them now in the back eddies on the rivers and creeks.
And I can see them now in the new-growth birch groves in forests.
And I can see them now in the faces of those walking through downtowns.
And I can see them now in the blazing orange fur of a newborn bison calf.
And I can see them now in the etchings on bull moose antlers.

Pretty soon you'll be able to see them too.

What Do You Believe In?

Do you believe in the ghosts of aunties and uncles that drive old single-bench pickup trucks spotted with bullet-hole rust, sweetgrass and beaded necklaces dangling from the rear-view mirror? Those who dream forever of empty stretches of prairie trail turned concrete road passed over by generations of everyone who held the memory of you close. Those who believed in you even when you didn't believe that the future could be infinite for all of us who live under and within endless sky, endless prairie wool, endless bison and endless coveys of sharptail grouse.

Do you believe in sitting on the shores of the Saskatchewan River next to nehiyawak cousins planning out the moose hunts that will keep meat flowing back into amiskwaciy-waskahikan for another winter so that all of our relations can taste the blood and body of a true Eucharist, the Earth made whole through the eyes of a two-year-old bull moose? His flesh sustaining and forever nurturing our kinship spirits that only move us further toward understanding who we were always meant to be.

Do you believe in the beauty of the wrinkles around an old lady's eyes while she sits wrapped up in a homemade quilt, sipping muskeg tea next to the wood-burning stove? Each line a thousand laughs, a thousand tears, a thousand stories spilled out so that we can move forward in a good way, holding truth next to our hearts, sustained through the crackle of birch burning dark into the night, forever holding onto our place next to the grandmothers who defined what it means to be family.

Do you believe in singing loud into the night? Barn dances replaced by pubs and karaoke machines. Potato champagne by cheap bottles of Pilsner. *Oh no, not I, I will survive, oh as long as I know how to love I know I'll stay alive* rippling through the air to the backdrop of fading fiddles, spoons, and the tapping of beer bottles on hardtop tables, cards swooshing as they're dealt high into the air. Bet on us, because we're not going anywhere. Never were, never will. Gloria Gaynor had it right all along.

Do you believe in those who aren't born yet? Those who will come after us. Those who will take back the land from the idea of Canada and give it away to the grasses. Eradicate the machinery, tear it down, build it up. Believe in the words and the way that pride is written all over the faces of those who learn what it means to own ourselves. To never bow under hell on earth. To never step back but always move forward knowing that within this landscape we are reborn, awoken, brought back by the artists and the writers, the poets and the dancers, the musicians and the lovers, the beaders and the hunters.

Because I do.

I believe in everything.

Acknowledgements

I would like to thank *The Malahat Review*, *The Fiddlehead*, *Grain*, *Prairie Fire*, *Mamawi Project* and *Hungry Zine* for publishing some of the poems in this collection and for giving space to my prairie musing. My agent, Cody Caetano, the crew at Nightwood Editions, and the staff at Glass Bookshop and Massy Books for the support. I'd like to thank jaye simpson, Emily Riddle, Molly Cross-Blanchard, Billy-Ray Belcourt, Jason Purcell, Chris Hutchinson and Matthew Weigel for reading earlier versions of this book and for the conversations around poetry practice and art. And as always, all the love to my friends and family and those who support my writing.

PHOTO CREDIT: ZACHARY AYOTTE

About the Author

Conor Kerr is a Métis Ukrainian writer. A member of the Métis Nation of Alberta, he is a descendant of the Lac Ste. Anne Métis and the Papaschase Cree Nation. His Ukrainian family are settlers in Treaty Four and Six territories in Saskatchewan. He likes to wrestle Labradors and wander around looking for birds. He was named a CBC writer to watch in 2022. He is the author of the poetry collection *An Explosion of Feathers* and the novel *Avenue of Champions*, which was shortlisted for the Amazon First Novel Award, won a 2022 ReLit Award and was longlisted for the 2022 Scotiabank Giller Prize.